IN A FIELD OF COTTON

MISSISSIPPI RIVER DELTA POEMS

LARRY D. THOMAS

2008 Texas Poet Laureate

Photographs by Jeffrey C. Alfier

BLUE HORSE PRESS REDONDO BEACH, CALIFORNIA 2019

IN A FIELD OF COTTON

MISSISSIPPI RIVER DELTA POEMS

LARRY D. THOMAS

2008 Texas Poet Laureate

Photographs by Jeffrey C. Alfier

Blue Horse Press
318 Avenue I # 760
Redondo Beach,
California 90277

Copyright © 2019 by Larry D. Thomas
All rights reserved
Printed in the United States of America

Cover art: Jeffrey C. Alfier,
"Tallahatchie County, Mississippi"

Editors: Jeffrey and Tobi Alfier
Blue Horse Press logo: Amy Lynn Hayes (1996)

ISBN 978-0-578-46620-0

No part of this book may be reproduced or transmitted in any form or by any means, electronic or mechanical, including photocopy, recording, or any information storage and retrieval system now known or to be invented, without permission in writing from the publisher, except by a reviewer who wishes to quote brief passages in connection with a review written for inclusion in a magazine, newspaper or broadcast.

FIRST EDITION © 2019

This and other Blue Horse Press Titles may be found at www.bluehorsepress.com

Full-length Poetry Collections by Larry D. Thomas

Amazing Grace (*Texas Review* Press 2001)

Where Skulls Speak Wind (*Texas Review* Press 2004)

Stark Beauty (Timberline Press 2005)

The Fraternity of Oblivion (Timberline Press 2008)

Larry D. Thomas: New and Selected Poems (Texas Christian University Press Texas Poets Laureate Series 2008)

The Skin of Light (Dalton Publishing 2010)

A Murder of Crows (Virtual Artists Collective 2011)

Uncle Ernest (Virtual Artists Collective 2013)

The Lobsterman's Dream: Poems of the Coast of Maine (El Grito del Lobo Press 2014)

As If Light Actually Matters: New & Selected Poems (*Texas Review* Press 2015)

Boiling It Down: The Electronic Poetry Chapbooks of Larry D. Thomas (Blue Horse Press 2019)

In memory of my parents and my grandparents

Contents

Preface

Acknowledgments

I. Staring Down the Dark

1. Chilly in the Silvery Fog
2. Old Houses
3. Photo: Rt. 24, Near Bayou Cane, LA
4. Boar
5. Photo: Helena, Arkansas
6. Sow
7. Blue Moon *(Helena-West Helena, Arkansas)*
8. Baby Ruth
9. Hard Wine
10. The Barbershop *(Orange Mound, Memphis, Tennessee)*
11. Photo: Greenwood, Mississippi

II. A White Cloud So Close to the Ground

15. Two Mules
16. The Plowman
17. Photo: Near St. James, LA
18. Hard Lines
19. Cotton
20. Photo: Gin Mill, Tallahatchie County, Mississippi

21. Hard Labor
22. Photo: Near French Settlement, LA
23. *Laundry Woman* (drawing by John Biggers)
24. The Wake *(Bolivar County, Mississippi, circa 1865)*

III. Aching for Tone

27. Pearl's Cotton Club *(for Pearl Murray, Blues Singer)*
28. Photo: Music Shop, Helena, Arkansas
29. Juke Joint *(vernacular term for an informal establishment featuring music and dancing)*
30. Photo: Blue Front Café, Bentonia, Mississippi
31. Lightnin' *(in memory of Samuel John "Lightnin'" Hopkins)*
32. Photo: My Place, Helena, Arkansas
33. Lifting Her Voice to God *(Plaquemines Parrish, LA)*
34. Photo: Country Church
35. Sweet Chariot
36. Photo: Crow with Abandoned Gin Mill, Thornton, Mississippi

Epilogue

39. Cotton

40. Appendix

43. About the Author and Photographer

Preface

I am inextricably connected to the Mississippi River Delta in spirit, emotion, and by bloodline. Three of my grandparents, born in western Tennessee around 1880 (my paternal grandfather was born in Texas; his father was born in Mississippi), migrated to west Texas in the late 1890s. They traveled by covered wagon. All four of them worked their entire lives as tenant cotton farmers, although my paternal grandfather was also a mule trader. They plowed the cotton fields with mules, and hand-picked the cotton as soon as it was ready for harvesting. My mother and father, who were thirty-nine and forty years of age, respectively, at the time of my birth, also hand-picked cotton into their late twenties until my father started working at a Mobil service station. From the early years of my childhood, I heard stories about my family's experiences on the tenant farms, and was fascinated by how they hand-picked cotton much like the black slaves on plantations throughout the American South. These stories made me feel a strong connection to blacks and black culture which I still feel to this day.

A significant development in my Delta experience occurred when, at the age of twenty (in 1967), I moved from west Texas where I was born and reared to the southeastern Texas city of Houston where I resided for forty-four years. The first thing I noticed about Houston was how deeply "Southern" it was. During my first year there, I became familiar with the music of the great Lightnin' Hopkins whose musical career blossomed in Houston in the 1940s. That was my introduction to "the blues" which quickly became, and still is to this day, one of my favorite musical genres.

What initially intrigued me about the blues genre was, among many other things, its evolution from Voodoo chants and spirituals to its undisputed stance as one of the original forms of authentic American music. Many of my fondest memories of my Houston years stem from the countless hours I spent soaking up the blues in the city's fascinating array of nightclubs which regularly featured live performances of blues greats, both established and up-and-coming.

Larry D. Thomas

Acknowledgments

Sincerest gratitude is extended to the publishers/editors of the publications noted below in which the poems and photographs indicated first appeared, sometimes in slightly different versions. Very special gratitude is extended to Jeffrey C. Alfier, founder, publisher, and co-editor of Blue Horse Press and the *San Pedro River Review*, for his splendid photography which graces the pages of this book.

Arkansas Review: A Journal of Delta Studies
   "Juke Joint *(vernacular term for an informal establishment featuring music and dancing)*," "Pearl's Cotton Club *(for Pearl Murray, Blues Singer)*," "Sweet Chariot," "The Wake *(Bolivar County, Mississippi, circa 1865)*," "Rt. 24, Near Bayou Cane, LA" (photo), "Near St. James, LA" (photo), and "Near French Settlement, Louisiana" (photo)

Callaloo: A Journal of African Diaspora Arts and Letters
   "Blue Moon *(Helena-West Helena, Arkansas)*"

CyberSoleil: A Literary Journal
   "Lifting Her Voice to God *(Plaquemines Parrish, Louisiana)*"

Down to the Dark River: An Anthology of Contemporary Poems about the Mississippi River, *Louisiana Literature* Press
    "Chilly in the Silvery Fog"

Elegant Rage: A Poetic Tribute to Woody Guthrie, Village Books Press
    "Hard Wine" and "The Plowman" ("The Plowman" was originally titled "The Ploughmen")

Mules and More Magazine
    "Two Mules"

Petrichor: word: //: image:
    "Baby Ruth"

REAL: Regarding Arts & Letters
    "Boar," "Old Houses" and "Sow"

Travelin' Music: A Poetic Tribute to Woody Guthrie, Village Books Press
    "Hard Labor" and "Hard Lines"

The Windhover: A Journal of Christian Literature
    "*Laundry Woman* (drawing by John Biggers)"

I. Staring Down the Dark

Chilly in the Silvery Fog

beginning to burn off,
I'm sitting on a bench
in Jackson Square, shortly
after sunrise. I can't

rid my mind of his visage,
the man in the Voodoo Museum
with the albino python
draped around his neck.

The ghost of voodooienne
Marie Laveau was palpable
throughout the place,
and I swear I saw her move

in her large portrait hanging
in the darkness. I will return
to the museum when it opens
for another careful look

at that painting. For now
I take deep breaths of the heavy,
humid air and I smell
the giant brown python

of the Mississippi sluicing
toward the Gulf, wearing down
the levee, shining and tumescent
with its meal of mice and men.

Old Houses

Bereft for decades of inhabitants,
they loom beneath the branches of ancient oaks
like mute matriarchs with arms crossed,

staring down the dark. When the wind blows,
wavy windowpanes clatter in their frames
like death rattles. The gables, embellished

with gingerbread, are iridescent and murmurous
with pigeons. In their grand, airy rooms,
haunted with the ghosts of a thousand stories,

shafts of moonshine come suddenly alive
with motes tumbling and spiraling like acrobats
in tiny, silent circuses of light.

Rt. 24, Near Bayou Cane, LA

Boar

Hair juts
from the sharp, black ridge
along his back,
stiff as rebar tips

in cured concrete.
His tusks,
tinged with blood
and gleaming in a shaft

of moonglow,
are the hooks
of Satan's grapnel.
Tough as a rugby football,

his stomach growls,
protuberant
with his suckling
sons and daughters.

Helena, Arkansas

Sow

Chomping her chocolates
of fresh road kills, she swaggers
through her slop, oblivious

of the piglets she crushed
during last night's slumber,
squishing through the splits

of her thick, cloven hooves.
The last boar which tried
to straddle her fabulous girth

fractured both forelegs.
She dined on his carcass
for days, grunting in the shade.

Blue Moon
(Helena-West Helena, Arkansas)

It sliced the horizon
like the toothed, spinning blade
of a silent table saw,

drawing her husband
to his boat. He knew
the fishing would be good that night.

She lost sight of him
several yards from the river's edge,
fighting the treacherous currents,

his shrunken silhouette
one with the indigo sky
he bled into like ink

into a blotter. He never returned.
For days, all she could eat was salads
she picked at with her fork,

staring riverward through the window
of a room lit with a shaft
of moonglow. Marbled with veins

of mold, even the cheese
she sprinkled over the fresh,
torn greens, was blue.

Baby Ruth

Though conceived by rape in a place where a thimbleful
of blackness was tantamount to the volume of a bushel,

her mother still carried her to term and had her
by natural childbirth. After the rape, her mother

was never the same, absentmindedly indulged in meth,
and passed the damage to the mind of Baby Ruth.

Despite the terrible odds against her, with God's grace,
Baby Ruth made it to adulthood, and with the optimal use

of compromised intelligence, earned her keep as the church's
cleaning lady. She still works there, left in her bléssed lurch

of gray, a strange angel absent either wing or horn
whose hands, groping in the darkness of rubber gloves, turn

filth into the immaculate conception of cleanliness,
leaving the sanctuary bejeweled with the bliss

of light flowing like waterfalls through panes of stained glass,
shattering the mirrors of pews with shotgun-blasted godliness.

Hard Wine

Their shotgun shacks
are hidden in the shadows
of skyscrapers,
their roof shingles
black as the ink
of desolate headlines.

Life drinks them
like hard wine
as crows' feet
deepen near their eyes.
Days, they labor
for bags of beans and rice,

and till little gardens
sparkling with shards
of broken glass.
Nights, in minutes
of hard-earned bliss,
their bedsprings creak

with the rhythm
of fine Swiss clocks
ticking their lives away,
ticking miles away
on the elegant mahogany
mantels of their bosses.

The Barbershop
(Orange Mound, Memphis, Tennessee)

The red and white stripes of the barber pole,
ever spiraling, symbolize the barber's
long-ago sideline of surgery. Every fortnight,
whether or not he needs a haircut
or really even a shave, the centenarian local

enters it, hangs his hat on the rack
inside the door, and seats himself
in the antique barber chair. The old barber
shakes his pinstriped cotton apron, and ties it
comfortably snug behind his customer's neck.

The whir of shears muffling his deepest terrors,
the local mumbles an old story in soft monotones
inaudible to the ears of the barber confidential
as the ears of a good reverend. His haircut
finished, and in the ultimate gesture of his trust,

he lays his weary head back, tightens his grip
on the arms of the barber chair, protrudes
his Adam's apple, and he waits
for the placement against his throat
of the stropped, gleaming blade of the razor.

Greenwood, Mississippi

II. A White Cloud So Close to the Ground

Two Mules

They work
sunrise to sunset
leaning into breezes
flaring their nostrils
with the breath of hell.

They wrench their hooves
from baking earth
only to sink them
over and over again,
pulling their stubborn plow.

Their broad backs
endure the whiplashes
of savage Delta sun
as their huge ears
ring with the music

of creaking harnesses
darkened with decades
of sweat-froth.
They plow on,
each the offspring

of a stud donkey
crossed
with a mare,
the last
of its noble kind.

The Plowman

His daughter,
to save herself from the black,
stampeding mares of the night,

clutches for dear life
her cotton-stuffed doll.
To endure the coming harvest,

he reads his Bible
paged with the skin of onions,
blows out his lantern

with the breath of fresh garlic,
and dangles carrots
from the rafters of his prayers.

In the heirloom
turnip watches of his master,
his hallowed lineage ticks.

Near St. James, LA

Hard Lines

At sunrise,
he takes his predetermined
place in the field, grips
the oaken handles of his plow,

and plods through the soil
in the musky wake of mules.
He keeps his rows
straight as the line

of his desire for sundown,
for the lantern-lit windows
of slave quarters
redolent with his wife

whose warm, enfolding flesh,
in his stolid, manly world
of iron and oak, is all
he'll ever know of softness.

Cotton

Like a white cloud
so close to the ground
it's stifling, it looms on the stalks
ready for picking. Thick brown stockings,
white, long-sleeved blouses buttoned at the throat,
and brown, ankle-length dresses of it
cling to the women's flesh like leeches.

When not picking it, they dream of it embroidered
into sterile, flawlessly symmetrical
little flowers, all the color they're allowed.
It snaps their bodies shut
like heirloom lockets their tiny photographs,
bodies they open but briefly in the darkness
and solely for the pleasure of the men.

Gin Mill, Tallahatchie County, Mississippi

Hard Labor

Her husband
and even the midwife tending her
so focused on her birthing him a son

they're deaf to the agony
of her third day of labor,
she whimpers little cries

the midwife muffles
with a damp, heavy cloth,
little cries creeping through the night

to the dark, freezing barn
where but the sows, mares, hens
and cows keep softly stirring.

Near French Settlement, Louisiana

Laundry Woman
(drawing by John Biggers)

She's flanked by the oak and iron pots
of brutal labor, in one of which
leans a washboard leading the eye

upward like a staircase to a backdrop
of clean clothes hanging on a line,
billowing in the breeze for stark contrast

to the tensile strength of the drawing's
heart of her massive hands and forearms,
rippling with tendon and muscle,

wrenching the dark decades, snapping
like matchwood the chains of slavery,
sketched for all time in graphite

everlasting as deep within the earth
a vein of ageless coal: soft, black,
and lustrous with the power of her soul.

The Wake
(Bolivar County, Mississippi, circa 1865)

Like the thief in the night
their Bibles promised, it came,
taking the young man's life

in the cotton field
with the burning venom
of a cottonmouth.

The grieving widows,
having long survived
their husbands, gathered

sans a word in the shotgun
shack to bathe the cold
corpse and lay it out

for burial. Day and night,
for three days, they tended it
as they had the others

so many times before,
the men off to the fields,
feigning Stoicism,

the aging widows left behind
to descend one at a time
the unforgiving rungs of death.

III. Aching for Tone

Pearl's Cotton Club
(for Pearl Murray, Blues Singer)

throbs in a night of knifings
where a distant siren
pierces the darkness
like a single note

wrenched from a singer's heart.
This is the haven of Pearl,
pulsing in the moonglow,
thick with the smoke of Kools,

Camels, bracing itself
for a flood of notes
of perfect pitch, blues-steeped,
dark, deep, the notes of a love

whose thrill is gone
welling in the soul of Pearl,
aching for tone
to free her from the spell.

Music Shop, Helena, Arkansas

Juke Joint
(vernacular term for an informal establishment featuring music and dancing)

Fashioned from a shotgun shack
flanking a huge field of cotton
and lit with Christmas lights,

it glowed in the darkness
like precious, moonlit stones
roiling in the palms of a gypsy.

On weekends, it pulsed with a crowd
of weary blacks, their sole refuge
from the giant, recalcitrant thumb

of the oppressive community at large.
From its precursors of black
folk rags and boogie woogie,

plucked from strings of baling wire
stretched taut across cigar box guitars,
the Delta blues emerged, coaxing patrons

to smile and dance, steeping their souls
in culture: beautiful, daunting, and sacred
as their heirloom African masks.

Blue Front Café, Bentonia, Mississippi

Lightnin'
(in memory of Samuel John "Lightnin'" Hopkins)

A soft guitar
loomed in the upper part of his windpipe,
lined with mucous membrane,

strung with two pairs of cords,
one above the other,
the upper pair false, doomed to silence,

the lower true, the fleshy,
expectant edges of which,
tensed or relaxed by the passage

of the airy fingers of a phantom,
produced the magical utterance
of the note.

My Place, Helena, Arkansas

Lifting Her Voice to God
(Plaquemines Parrish, Louisiana)

The immaculate pleats of her robe
belie the loose, wrinkled flesh beneath it,
her gloves the artifacts of hands

arthritic from decades of domestic labor.
Eighty if a day, every Sunday morning,
she ascends the steps to the choir loft,

and assumes her place on the makeshift bleachers.
Fixing her bright, bespectacled eyes on the baton,
she waits for its first, sparrow-quick dip,

and, in a single motion, drops her mandible
and belts out a note of flawless tremolo,
a note of such powerful purity

it all but shatters the panes of stained glass
radiant as the raspberry sun which, a century
before and but a mile from where she sings,

down through the branches of an ancient live oak,
bathed with God's good grace the pendulous,
soul-freed body of her grandfather.

Country Church

Sweet Chariot

In his nursing home bed,
he burns the midnight oil

of feverish sleep.
His fingertips are calloused

from countless hours
of strumming the baling wire

of cigar box guitars.
With legs of nothing but bones

draped with thin, chocolate satin,
he kicks the cotton covers to the floor,

and lies prostrate in a field of cotton
ready for harvest, the endless rows

the staves of hymns
cradling the notes of his soul.

Crow with Abandoned Gin Mill, Thornton, Mississippi

Epilogue

Cotton

It blanketed Mother
in the pale blue
softness of a nightgown;
Dad, the propriety
of a white shirt.

At their request,
even their caskets
were fashioned of it
to aid their swift
reunion with the earth.

For miles around
the cemetery,
red fields of it
lay fallow, fields
where in their youth,

sunup to sundown,
they picked it, each
a hundred pounds a day,
where they picked it
till their fingers bled.

(from *Stark Beauty*, Timberline Press 2005)

Appendix

A critical essay regarding Thomas's Delta poetry titled, "Despair and Hope through Delta Labor in the Poetry of Larry D. Thomas," by J. Todd Hawkins, appeared in the *Arkansas Review: A Journal of Delta Studies*, Volume 50, Issue 1.

Additional poems by Thomas which were inspired by the Mississippi River Delta and which appear in several of his previous books include the following:

"Tumescence," "The Azaleas" and "Of Crows and Cornfields," **Amazing Grace** (*Texas Review* Press 2001);

"In the Voodoo Lounge" and "Twin Spinsters in Blue," **The Woodlanders** (Pecan Grove Press 2002);

"Grandmother Worrell," "Grandmother Thomas," "Mule Trader" and "Jake," **Where Skulls Speak Wind** (*Texas Review* Press 2004);

"Scarecrows," "Cotton" and "The Sandstorm," **Stark Beauty** (Timberline Press 2005);

"French Quarter," **Larry D. Thomas: New and Selected Poems** (TCU Press Texas Poets Laureate Series 2008);

"Cicadas," **Dark Pearls** (LaNana Creek Press/Stephen F. Austin State University Press 2009);

"Holdout," **The Skin of Light** (Dalton Publishing 2010);

"Stained Overalls," "Deep Blues" and "Fresh Fried Chicken," ***Uncle Ernest*** (Virtual Artists Collective 2013);

"*Heading for the Higher Paying Jobs* (by Thornton Dial, High Museum of Art, Atlanta, Georgia)," ***Art Museums*** (Blue Horse Press 2014);

"*Shotguns, 1987*," "Harmonica" and "Mama Sug," ***As If Light Actually Matters: New & Selected Poems*** (*Texas Review* Press 2015); "Mama Sug" was first published in an e-chapbook titled *Five Lavender Minutes of an Afternoon* (*Right Hand Pointing* 2010); and

"Waiting 'Round to Die (song by Townes Van Zandt)," published with the title "Cleatus Muses," ***Boiling It Down: The Electronic Poetry Chapbooks of Larry D. Thomas*** (Blue Horse Press 2019); first published in an e-chapbook titled *Pecos* (*Right Hand Pointing* 2017).

About the Author

Larry D. Thomas, a member of the Texas Institute of Letters and the 2008 Texas Poet Laureate, has published several award-winning and critically acclaimed collections of poetry, most recently *As If Light Actually Matters: New & Selected Poems* (*Texas Review* Press/Texas A&M University Press Consortium 2015) and *Boiling It Down: The Electronic Poetry Chapbooks of Larry D. Thomas* (Blue Horse Press 2019). Among the awards he has received for his poetry are two *Texas Review* Poetry Prizes (2001 and 2004), the 2004 Violet Crown Book Award (Writers' League of Texas), two Western Heritage Awards (National Cowboy & Western Heritage Museum), a 2007 Poets' Prize nomination (Nicholas Roerich Museum), and eight nominations for the Pushcart Prize. Thomas's Mississippi River Delta poems have appeared in eleven of his published books and in numerous national literary journals including the *Arkansas Review: A Journal of Delta Studies*, *Callaloo: A Journal of African Diaspora Arts and Letters*, and *The Windhover: A Journal of Christian Literature*. Anthologies in which his Delta poems appear include *Down to the Dark River: An Anthology of Contemporary Mississippi River Poems* (*Louisiana Literature* Press) and *The Southern Poetry Anthology, Volume VIII: Texas* (*Texas Review* Press). Three of Thomas's grandparents and his paternal great-grandfather were born in the Delta and reared there until they moved to west Texas in the late 1800s.

About the Photographer

Jeffrey C. Alfier is 2018 winner of the Angela Consolo Manckiewick Poetry Prize, from Lummox Press. In 2014, he won the Kithara Book Prize, judged by Dennis Maloney. Poetry and photography credits include *Crab Orchard Review*, *Arkansas Review*, *Atlanta Review*, *The Carolina Quarterly*, *Columbia College Literary Review*, *Copper Nickel*, *december magazine*, *Emerson Review*, *Iron Horse Literary Review*, *Kestrel*, *Gargoyle*, *Hotel Amerika*, *Louisville Review*, *Permafrost*, *Poetry Ireland Review*, *South Carolina Review*, *Southern Poetry Review*, *Southwestern American Literature*, *The Stinging Fly* and *Texas Review*. He is author of several poetry books, including *The Wolf Yearling, Idyll for a Vanishing*

River, Fugue for a Desert Mountain, Anthem for Pacific Avenue: California Poems, Southbound Express to Bayhead: New Jersey Poems, The Red Stag at Carrbridge: Scotland Poems, Bleak Music (a photo and poetry collaboration with poet Larry D. Thomas), *The Storm Petrel: Poems of Ireland* and *The Color of Forgiveness* (co-authored with fellow editor Tobi Alfier). *Gone This Long: Southern Poems*, is forthcoming from Main Street Rag Publishing.

www.ingramcontent.com/pod-product-compliance
Lightning Source LLC
LaVergne TN
LVHW010034070426
835510LV00006B/129